Moments of the Soul

poems of meditation and mindfulness
by writers of every faith
2010

To Susan —

With soulful love,

Nancy Priff

Published by Spirit First
PO Box 8076
Langley Park, Maryland 20787
www.SpiritFirst.org

Published October 2010

Printed in the United States of America

Cover photograph by Marc Goldring

Moments of the Soul: poems of meditation and mindfulness by writers of every faith 2010
—1st edition

ISBN 978-0-9800314-1-6

10 9 8 7 6 5 4 3 2 1

First Edition

## Dedication

This book is dedicated to everyone who takes time to sit
for a moment of silence and stillness

To Heather, Jeremiah, Eric, and Ashley
for being part of who I am

To ehj2 for helping make this book happen

To Sami and Don for lovingly encouraging me

To Oprah, for always reminding me to do the inner work
and always inspiring me to live my best life

thank you
diana christine

<u>iv</u>
Moments of the Soul

# Contents

Moments of the Soul

Moments of the Soul

This book was made possible with the generous participation of the following people. Thank you, all.

All participants in our Spirit First Poetry Contest 2010 and all your beautiful writing

Our Spirit First poetry contest judging committee (anonymous but very deeply appreciated)

Marc Goldring for your cover photography, your ISBN, and your poetry review

Cindy Lee Jones, Ashley Litecky, Paula Basile, and Wendy Winn for your photography in our book's interior

Betty Paugh Ortiz for your special edit and Danielle Reyes for making it happen

Webmaster Win Singleton for keeping us connected

Harkirat Singh for supporting the work of Spirit First, always and with so much love.

Moments of the Soul

<u>x</u>
Moments of the Soul

## Introduction

People often ask me "What is meditation?" and "What does meditation feel like?" These are big questions, and important ones, but it can be difficult to put a spiritual experience into words for another to be able to taste and feel. Can we bring someone else into our practice of meditation? Is it possible to share with another our very own moments of the soul? The writers of this book have attempted to do just this, and the rest of us hold in our hands the opportunity to feel what they feel in their most holy places.

Read the opening lines of Wendy Winn's poem "Free for all" as she begins to speak to us in the simplest way possible to express what meditation is like:

> *There was a performance artist, Bill Harding,*
> *Who used to carry about a briefcase filled with sod.*
> *He'd surprise everyone by opening it,*
> *Setting it down, removing his shoes, and stepping into his*
> *Own private park.*
> *Meditation's like that.*

Wendy's poem continues with other real-life images to illustrate meditation, and as many times as I have read her words (even several times aloud before audiences), I still find my eyes wet with tears by the time I reach the end...

> *It's all yours. It's all mine.*
> *Any time.*
> *Meditation's like that.*

Moments of the Soul

And it's true, for all of us, always there, always available, always waiting, as Melinda Coppola describes in her poem "Say Yes":

> *...in the soul of your soul,*
> *that place where the still pond waits*
> *like a lover, to come home to over and over and*
> *to slip into like a deep silent dream, that quiet water*
> *reflecting your grace.*

Do you feel the longing for this quiet place? Can you tell of this hunger? Read the words of Christina Beasley in her poem "where silence grows":

> *i want to be still but not how*
> *a dead thing is. not stale or pallid,*
> *like worn paint. i want to know*
> *the way that vibrancy can tiptoe*
> *through the veins of my palms; serene*
> *and cool, humming a song of smoke*
> *and light.*

Some of the poems open with words that nourish me for many days and others close with final words that leave me breathless, as in Temple Cone's poem "If There's a Resurrection":

> *If there's a resurrection, God shall join us quietly by the*
> *fireside.*
> *From his hands tumble flowers of amen as intricate as*
> *Persian epics.*

Moments of the Soul

*From his lips pour waters of forgiveness, which he too shall
drink.*

The poems in this book came into being from a call for
submissions that went out in our first annual Spirit First
poetry contest, asking for poems on the themes of
meditation, mindfulness, silence, stillness, and solitude.

We received 741 poems from 42 states and 23 foreign
countries, poems from writers who are Buddhist,
Christian, Jewish, Islamic, Hindu…and many others
including those whose practices do not follow an
organized religion. Meditation and mindfulness are not
about doctrine but are about personal experience, and we
are honored to have the words of so many writers from
so many walks of life.

We are grateful to everyone who participated, including
those who sent beautiful and profound works that are not
included in this first collection. Everyone who
participated is part of the light of the whole, and we thank
you for your presence.

And now, in the words of Darrell Lindsey in his poem
"AMness":

*I have found a fragrance in meditation tonight…*

I hope you find a beautiful, sweet fragrance in your
reading of meditation poetry in this book.

Moments of the Soul

All proceeds from this book go to
Spirit First, which will one day be
Spirit First Meditation Retreat Center
with quiet walking trails, fragrant gardens,
and places to pause that include Buddhist, Christian,
Islamic, Hindu, and Jewish sanctuaries.

Moments of the Soul

Moments of the Soul

Moments of the Soul


poems of meditation and mindfulness
by writers of every faith
2010


edited by Diana Christine Woods

<u>2</u>
Moments of the Soul

# Mindfulness

*Photography by Cindy Lee Jones*

# Unless you

Drew Myron

Unless you

visit the dark places, you'll never
feel the sea pull you in and under,
swallowing words before they form.
Until you visit places within you
cloistered and constant, you will travel
in a tourist daze, wrought with too much
of what endures, depletes.

If you never turn from light, close
your eyes, feel the life inside, you'll leave
the church, the beach, your self,
knowing nothing more.

Unless you are mute, you will not
know your urgent heart, how it beats
between the thin skin of yes and no.

*Winner, First-Place*
*Spirit First Poetry Contest 2010*

# Koan

Iain Macdonald


I wish that when
I watch the Great Blue Heron
catch its prey
I would not at once
start forming phrases
like "garden statue stance,"
or think
of Mary Oliver's poem
*The Egret*,
in which she asks,
"What is this white death
that opens like a dark door?"

I wish
that I could simply see
the heron catch its prey
without seeking
ways to capture
what it looks and feels like
watching the heron
catch its prey.

# My Dog Has Buddha Nature

Bill Frayer

More than my Buddha,
My little dog
Waiting for a scrap
Teaches me more about living
In the present moment.

Her face intent, her gaze focused
As in meditation upon the morsel
Of toast, for which she has learned
She has a reasonable expectation
Of success.

The next moment, the toast gone,
She plops down
Slipping into a new present moment,
Asleep at once.

Or, sitting, attuned to sound
Inaudible to me, still
Timeless as a sphinx
Patient.

Were that I could emulate
Her mindful presence.

My curse of self awareness
Dominates my waking moments

Centering on my restless head
Which keeps me from the now
And present to my senses
Blocking access to my deepest
Most resplendent center.

Siddhartha understood my dog
And how our evolution
Made us fit to prosper
But guaranteed
Our discontent.

# Rerouting the Driver

Mary Gilliland


Like the chauffeur of a car that never stalls
part of my brain plans which way to turn at the next
corner,
when to refill the tank,
how to avoid radar, push the limit without a ticket.

She's always ahead of me
testing out alternative routes,
digesting the meal before I eat it.
If I order a vacation, forced retirement,
she races, claims a little work today
will help the wheels run smoothly.
If I scream that I can drive myself
without a body blocking the view,
she fervently answers that someone
must see to business, tinker, think ahead.

Before the next long drive, the next escape into spinning
a new project, the next detour from recollection,
I'll sugar that chauffeur's tank.
The wheels, always going nowhere,
really won't.

Look at the light changing red to green.
Look at her eyes, their color restored, blinking loudly.
Seized pistons have fractured her glare at the endless
road;

she's left the machine, its door hung open to rust in the rain.
Look inside the crossroads cafe:
I'm finishing my leftovers among bright lights and tablecloths;
she's drinking a steamy cup of the present.

Moments of the Soul

# Stone Mind

A. Jarrell Hayes

Enter the mind of wood,
Not of treetops
And leaves swaying in the wind,
But sturdy trunks
Which remain unmoving
And split all that rush
Against its rough bark.

Better yet,
Possess the mind of rock,
The stubbornness of stone
Mountains piercing the heavens
And slicing clouds,
Causing the insubstantial
Puffs to bleed snow and ice
Upon the tip of the blade.

Remain still and do not move –
Like wood and rock –
And the world will melt
Away
In the presence
Of your fortitude.

# The Fan

Allene Rasmussen Nichols

The fan's center
must not move,
must hold the bolts,
must stand alone,
in the shadow of the blades.

On hot summer days,
when the fan stirs
the thick air
and chases condensations
up the sides of water glasses,
that which moves
holds stillness in its heart.

# Watering the Plants

Wayne Lee

It is a simple thing,
watering the household plants.
It can be done without mind.
But then one would miss
drawing the tepid water
from the kitchen tap,
filling the ceremonial jar,
soaking the soil and feeding
the roots, turning the pots
to meet the sun, spraying
the leaves, breathing in
the perfume of fertility.
All I ask is to be aware.

# Mindfulness Reminder

Iain Macdonald

One moment
to let the razor slip;
five minutes
to stop the bleeding.

# Don't Invite Your Thoughts to Tea

Marie-Elizabeth Mali

I ask them to leave. They turn
away but don't budge. Pretty soon,
Not-Good-Enough starts a conversation
with I'm-the-Best but they get stuck
on introductions. At-One-With-Everything
looks around for someone to talk to
that's not her. Be-A-Good-Hostess hands me
a used cup. Pushing around little triangles
of cucumber sandwich, I-Want-Chocolate
speaks up. I repeat they all have to leave.
You're-An-Idiot gestures he's got something
to tell me. I say we have to learn to work
together. Here-We-Go-Again sighs and rolls
her eyes. The rest sink into cushions,
refusing to leave space for Silence to preside.

# The Call of Silence

Veronica Bowman


Silence beckons.
I answer and
I am rewarded with moments of tranquility
that can be found only when surrounded by silence.
Silence encourages me
to intentionally engage in the art of doing nothing.
In the silence, nothingness becomes something
of a world all its own.
Beauty is magnified.
Serenity surrounds me and
I become mindfully aware of the inner peace
that can be found only when I answer
the summons of silence.

# When the Audience Forgets

Mary Elizabeth Anderson


Left alone with my thoughts,
I watch them audition.

They prefer the drama
that ensues
when the audience forgets
that this is only a play.

That's when they feel alive.
That's when they feel important.
That's when they feel—
Real.

The illusion
depends on the darkness
in the theatre.

But when the house lights come up,
the audience disbands,
the illusion evaporates, and

Only the director is—
One with the silence.

# Awake

Caitlin Gildrien

Morning sits.

The bell comes,
louder than the creek.
We tumble into our brains –
hardly have the echoes faded
and I am babbling. Silent,
but babbling.

The jays repeat
their morning mantra.

I greet my fear,
my desire,
my anxious mind:
Am I late?
Too early? Will my feet smell,
and what socks to wear,
will I have coffee, or tea?
Will he smile at me, and
will I smile back?

Not until the end bell rings
do I realize

I am awake.

# How Hannah stopped the waterfall

Wendy Winn

Hannah's like I can't believe I have to work late just
because she's off skiing, I mean I've got three kids and
even coming home at 5 is late enough and I'm probably
not going to be home till 7 and when I get the groceries
and those kids they don't help for nothing and

Instead of echoing her worries and her stress and talking
bad about her coworker who has the audacity to go on a
vacation I say

Hannah, stop.
Hannah, breathe.

Hannah slows the flow of the verbal waterfall and it starts
to just trickle well the money's good the overtime but I
can't stand to be cooped up in that office 10 hours a day
and then when I get home there's a whole nother day's
work to do the laundry and the dishes and

And I don't chip in and say yes, that's right, life's hard, I
say

Hannah, slow down,
Hannah, breathe.

By now Hannah's stopped the river's flow and she's just
waiting, she's listening. She's quiet.

Hannah, I say.
Hannah.
Take five, or ten. Just take them. Grab them out of the air, squeeze them in. Just when you don't think you have them, that's when you need them most.

Hannah's just listening, she's quiet.

Hannah.
Find yourself a little quiet place. I don't care if it's in the bathroom. In the closet.
Just find it.
Take yourself a little candle if you have one, and light it, and just squint your eyes and look at that dancing flame. Just focus on the flame, and begin to feel yourself breathing. The miraculous, always present breath you don't ever have to think about. Just feel it slowly going in, slowly going out. Just be.

I hear Hannah stirring something, moving pots and pans.

Hannah? Listen, it's just for 10 minutes. Go shut your eyes. Shut down. Look inward. If a thought drifts in, just gently shoo it away like a fly in August. Don't pay any attention to it, just whisk it away. You do this a couple of days, and you call me back.

I don't hear any more dishes. Don't hear anything at all.

Okay, she says, sounding like the last of the air escaping a worn out balloon, a little disappointed I didn't slam her coworker or join her in bashing her entire crummy life.

19
Moments of the Soul

Everyone likes people to take their side, even if they're on the wrong one, even if they're aren't really any sides at all.

Three days later the phone rings.

Hey you, Hannah says.

I'm surprised it ends there, no waterfall, no gushing. Very un-Hannah like.

Hey you, Hannah says, gently, softly, centered. Thanks.

# Into the Now

Norma Laughter

He sits,
exuding tranquility.
We sit,
learning stillness.
Odd
we should need guidance
to be
here
now.
Yet out there
it takes
stubbing a toe,
breathtaking beauty,
a car crash –
pain, awe, shock,
to call down our thoughts
and immerse us
in the immediate.
Grow roots
into awareness,
he says,
into presence.
Open every moment
and you won't miss a thing.

# Blessing XXXV

Anne Whitehouse

Slowly I'm achieving
a baby's perfect posture,
when it learns to sit
without any strain,
shoulder blades
pressing into the back
like folded wings,
the shoulders back, too,
the crown of the head
over the soft palate and throat,
in line with the heart
down to the pelvic floor,
seat of the body.

My body fills with breath,
my heart at front and center,
thoughts dissolved,
softening, deepening
into the interval
where a goddess passes by.

# Prayer to be Reverent in the Present

Mary Dyer Hubbard

Loving God,
It's so hard for me
to be *in the now*.
My mind, like a dragonfly on a pond,
skitters from one distraction to the next.
What I really want,
is to sit by that pond in peaceful stillness,
drinking in the sunlight and its sparkle-dance across the
water.
I want to see people that way too,
with reverence, awe and delight
at your amazing creation.
Let my eyes ask their eyes if I may come in.
If not, may peace be with that one
who isn't up for company right now.
And then there's me.
Help me hold myself with tenderness
as if a precious and delicate vase
with tiny crackles etched on its transparent surface.
So many flaws, yet so beautiful,
empty to receive the abundance of your love
in every now moment.

$\underline{24}$

Moments of the Soul

# Personal Practice

*Photograph of Yogini Ashley Litecky*

# A Free for All

Wendy Winn

There was a performance artist, Bill Harding,
Who used to carry about a briefcase filled with sod.
He'd surprise everyone by opening it,
Setting it down, removing his shoes, and stepping into his
Own private park.
Meditation's like that.

My parents used to fly private airplanes.
It always amazed me that down here it could be
Grey and miserable and full of car horns and traffic lights
And up there, up past the clouds,
Petty problems disappeared and everything was always
peaceful.
Meditation's like that.

You've maybe heard about creating a special place
To hold in your mind, at the dentist's, in traffic,
under stress.
I used to always use the linens department at Sears
or Penney's.
Among soft folded towels in coral and turquoise,
Among display beds piled high with throw pillows and
matching comforters,
Who could be worried?
Meditation's like that.

Your own private park you can slip off to
whenever you need
A quiet moment to reconnect to the Earth and
all that turns with it
and all it turns in.
Your own blue sky above the rain clouds you can fly
off to whenever you need
To rise above the trivial rain showers of the day to day,
to become the sky itself.
Your own perfect image of calm and order,
not necessitating terrycloth or combed cotton
or 100% down
a realization that everything is in its perfect
place and time,
including you.

It's all yours. It's all mine.
Any time.
Meditation's like that.


*Winner, Second Place*
*Spirit First Poetry Contest 2010*

# Evening Meditation

Iain Macdonald

We walk
straight into a setting sun
so fierce
that, near-blind,
we must lower our heads
and slow our pace
until the world narrows
to what is immediately before us,
which we approach,
encounter,
and leave
one careful step
at a time.

# Thor Ballylee

Diane Kendig

After standing in Yeats's long shadow
in a Dublin park, where he stood, both of us
heavy, in loose earthen garb, having lost
two dearest, one dead and the other
in love with another, escaping our strife,
I arrived at the home of the unrequited lover.

I wept by the plaque marking the place.
Then, I climbed the tower.
I did not climb into his bed
as another writer told me she did.
I did not punch the buttons to hear
sonorous voices intoning his poems
against the corkscrew stone stairs
up to the parapet.

I climbed in the echo of my own steps
circling to arrive where all around
I saw kilometers of green, blotted with white
so far off I couldn't hear the bleating,
could not hear anything animal, nor
human, so far below, not a car
on gravel even. Not even wind.
Just a deep quiet, as of sleep, of rest.
I did not weep then but descended,
ready for whatever would come next.

Moments of the Soul

# Temporary Autonomous Zone

Gabriel Griffin

*They* have no idea I'm here!
No, they think I'm trotting
Round the shops or stopping off
At that nice doc's!

*They'll* never guess I'm here
Away from them, in this sacred wood
Alone, niftily pick-pocketing time,
Stealing moments of my own.

*They'll* never find me here, not think
To look in these old trees, this bit of land forgotten,
Jammed between the abandoned school
And the new road's muddy cutting.

Here I sit on ancient stone
Doing sod all, whilst *they*
Worry up and down around the home,
Hunt and call through the exploding town.

*They* won't guess where I am! *They'll* think I'm just
Forgetful, late, or, perhaps, come over queer.
Instead, I'm *here* where black birds plunder scarlet berries,
Crunching oak-leaves rimed with host-white hoar.

Here with silent laugh I sip the grail of solitude,
That treasure *they'll* not think to hunt or find.

And when I go, I'll take back with me stolen fruits
To fly me through the parched and shouting nights.

# Susurration

Stephen Mead


The Bell of Mindfulness
is what Buddhism tells of
for us seeking peace
as a forehead hand.
Yours is laid blue
as a dove's shadow
and from it comes the quiet
where I can hear song
as prayers.
Then the visions come
true as stepping stones
just barely visible
under rapids.
This name, that
catches up to the faces
as breeze to leaves
in the reeds of these bones.
Blow on souls
so that my own
spirit's straw
turns to transparent pewter
and tongue in the mouth of god.

# Havdalah

Lorri B. Danzig

Magic and mystery
fill this time of transition
when the toes of one foot
still dangle in the sea
of the sacred, while the
mind races to embrace
the ordinary litany of life.

Heart open, face uplifted
reluctant to release my hold
on the Holy, I let myself
fall into the night sky, and then
aglow with God-light, I count
the three stars that signal
a return of the ordinary.

# Zazen

Caitlin Gildrien

There beneath the bodhi tree,
he cradled me in his lap.
Fed me yogurt and rice
from his fingers,
brought me back to life. I was starving.
I suckled those dark fingers,
dripping honey,
dripping salt,

I watched the sun
move through the leaves.
My eyes focused.

My eyes opened.
The creek was full of
clear water nearby.
It smelled of sulfur,
it smelled of citrus,
roses, incense, and death.

Fruit grew ripe, split
along its swollen skin, was eaten
by the screaming birds. Still he fed me.

Soon I could walk. Soon I walked
away. My belly rounded, my feet bare.
I was gone a long time. Then

came back to sit beside him.
Watched the moon move through the branches,
dripping nectar,
dripping blood. I was thirsty.
I drank deep.

He fed me from his fingers, gently.
We watched the morning star.

# Failed Meditation

Liz Ahl

*The greatest effort is not concerned with results.*
*The greatest meditation is a mind that lets go.*
*~ Atisha*

I want to open the book of peace
and read all the signs left for me there,
but this wanting is a bad translation
against my broken tongue.

I want to find the room inside the apple
where stars are born, but I choke
on the seeds of this wanting.

I want to plunder the treasure chest of peace,
but this wanting snaps off
in the padlock's tiny aperture.

I want the twitching sparrow in my heart
to explode into flight from its branch,
but my wanting salts its folded wings.

I draw each *om* from my pocket
like a brass subway token
but none of the express trains
stop at this station of my wanting.

I drop lacquered *mala* beads one by one

into each pearly chamber of the nautilus,
and am entranced by the clatter and echo
of my wanting.

I want to stroke the cool curve of peace,
to rest my cheek against its resonant belly,
to know its circumference –
but the wanting puts my nerves to sleep.

And so I embrace this wanting, wake again
into its steady backache, don its ochre robes
of pathos. It is my suffering.
Because I know it, it is almost peace.

# Evening Grace

Krista Kurth


Sitting down at the kitchen table,
A warm plate of freshly cooked
Food before me - pausing
To prepare to give thanks for the day,
All of a sudden I see that ease
Has crept in – all on its own –
And begun to find a home
In the body of my life,
Without me knowing it had arrived.

Breathing in, I feel
Tiny tendrils of peace
Twirling and opening out,
Taking root, in the new found
Space in my day - in my heart -
Spreading warm comfort
Throughout - and - into my core,
And with it ripples
Of expanding quiet joy.

Breathing out, I feel
Already full.
Bowing my head
I take hold of the loving hand
Reaching out for mine.
In silent gratitude, I welcome
This easy peace,

Moments of the Soul

And my Self,
Home.

Moments of the Soul

# Falling for God

Lisa Dordal

It's an odd thing
to wake up, as I did,
screaming, letting
the God I didn't believe in
have it, every cell,
every vein, every
sinew, shouting,
again and again,
from my rented bed,
in my rented flat, aching
for my false gods of security –
my husband, our house,
the daughter I was
certain would be ours, one day –
odder still to hear,
in return, silence,
to hear it become
its own

      rich

         thing.

# Silent Places

Allene Rasmussen Nichols

I need those silent places
within and without
where I can feel my body
expand and contract
with the
breath
that sustains me
and where
the softness of the pillow
under my hands
is as important
as the web
of the wider world
with its bullying
and braying governments
and angry honking cars
and endless
noise.

# After the Meditation Retreat

Michelle Demers

A week's worth of laundry.
Weeds – hundreds of them.
No food in the refrigerator.
Pounding rain that seeps down the chimney.
Mail that hasn't been answered.
Yearning for the simple monk's room.
The cat's full litter box.
Newspapers stacked up.
Words of the guru floating through my mind.
Answering machine blinking.
The lilacs' intoxicating fragrance.
Traffic.
Memories of the dream-like misty sunset over the river.
> A vague, fleeting remembrance of the yes, the ah,
> the sweetness,
> the fullness, the emptiness.
The rotten pear in the fruit bin.
The abyss of silence.
All of it sacred, awake.

# Conundrum

Gill Dobson

Evening shadows fall,
Softening shapes and colours;
Grey in all its shades descends,
Deepening slowly
To a rich velvety black.

Stillness;
Starlight;
Silver moon rising
Over the earth void;
Where hours before
Trees and houses and cars,
Children on bicycles,
Jogging men and gossiping women
Cluttered the space
With form and noise and busyness.

My thoughts merge slowly
Into the darkness,
Becoming one
With the blessed emptiness
As cares and worries fade.

Loving Lord
Light of my life,
Lover of my soul,
Comes quietly

To meet me,
Wrapping my mind
With grace and peace and joy,
Dissolving my daylight doubts and distresses
In the deepness of His being.

I bend my head
And open my heart;
Quiet words,
Suffused with hope,
Whisper a prayer into the silent night.

Heart beats;
Hope rises;
He hears
And speaks His silent grace
Into my soul anew,
Lifting me out
Of the daylight darkness
To the place where the hope flame flickers and flares,
Illuminating my subterranean soul.

I close my eyes
And sleep comes,
Drawing me in
To that place of refreshing
Where dreams are sweet and He holds me safe.

Darkness dissipates;
Dawn breaks and
Daylight rises,
And I stretch

Moments of the Soul

And greet the risen morn,
Savouring my reborn being
And the promise of His light-bearing presence
Through all the now-shadowed challenges of this new-
made day.

Moments of the Soul

# That Kind of Rain

Maria Wingfield Butler

I'm talking about the rain
that softened the earth
that drank it in for a long week,
that brought me inside
thinking *I'm a drop*
that falls to flow with others dropping,
connected, moving without mind.

When it is my time to die,
I want to join the others
flowing in an ocean of souls
on a warm day
in a sea of
September tide,
becoming one again.

I'll need the sun at last
to ripple across the water
casting a rainbow
arching the dunes,
like the signature of God
signing me in again.

# Labyrinth

Peter Huggins


The labyrinth at Amiens
Cathedral is octagonal,
A black path set

In green marble.
It is a spiritual place
Inside a spiritual place.

When I find it,
I step inside and I walk
Its turnings, taking

With me all that I am.
I leave nothing outside.
I follow the path

To the center and feel
I have opened a door
Into myself:

I have crossed
Thin space and stepped
Into the divine.

# Fuga Mundi

Christine Riddle

I climb the stone steps,
edges smoothed and treads worn low by
generations of (mostly) faithful feet.
Some came jubilant,
some heavy hearted,
some merely obedient;
newlyweds in showers of rice,
newly bereaved in fresh pain,
newborns in christening robes.
Those in need of absolution.
Others who prayed for intercession.
I come simply for meditation.

I prefer church midday, midweek.
No fussy toddlers, no clanging bells,
no thunderous chords, no unison prayers.
Suspended in my cool, dim refuge,
bright heat and traffic noise sealed out,
it's as if the space itself is holding its breath.

My eyes adjust as I unconsciously
dip my fingers in the font and make
the sign of the cross—old habit.
Gleaming sinners turned saints cast rainbows on the
polished pews.
Plaster icons smile benevolently, illuminated by flickering
votives.

Beside the altar a vigil light glows red,
signifying "Divine Presence."
The faint smell of beeswax mingled with incense
and a forgotten prayer card
are the only reminders of yesterday's funeral mass.
From the shadowy transept, the echo of a muffled cough
ricochets between marble and brass, filling the cavernous
vault.

I lean back and look up at the azure dome
crowded with cherubim and seraphim,
and bearded patriarchs, gilt
halos dull with age.
It's quiet again ... my breathing slows ... my eyes soften.
The only sound is the hushed click of rosary beads.

# Quaker Meeting

Carol F. Peck

Enter the silence of Meeting
Week after week after week,
Hear the peace growing around you,
Leading to answers you seek;
Reach, reach for your center,
Search with your inner sight,
Feel the communion of stillness,
Touch the tranquil Light.

When you go out of the Meeting
Into the work of the day,
Sometimes the noise and confusion
Unsettle you, get in your way;
But if you will reach for your center
To capture the peace anew,
You'll find that the silence of Meeting
Has entered you.

*Note: This was originally a song. Music is available upon request by contacting the author at* <u>cfpeckprod@aol.com</u>

# Two Girls in Church

Lisa Dordal


Sitting thigh to thigh, socks swinging.
One with hair the orange of December squash,
the other's white as moths' wings.
Each leafing through the musty pages of Service –
pressed and sung by the many before –
one turns to the other, saying:
*Smell my breath* and pushes out air
through the hard, smooth roundness of candied fire.
The other grins and delights, while, one pew back,
my awe grows wide to welcome in
the sundry smells of gathered saints –
drawing deep the God who breathes the same, to us.

# Church, Front Row

Janet McCann


Church, front row, far right
behind the crèche, I see Joseph's
shoulder and the Christ child's head
and the priest's hands through
the front opening of the stable,
framed in knotty wood. I like
this perspective, available
only to a latecomer:

priest's hands holding
paten, chalice, the ritual
performed a few feet from my
nose and right above the head
of baby Jesus in the crèche.
Paint peels off the wooden sheep.
I watch the altar boy
ring the bells, I could reach out

and touch him, there are four
bells attached to the wooden handle.
Now I look at the big Nikes
under the white robes of the
boys. Their faces composed,
distant, as though they were looking
into eternity as they gently touched
things of the ritual, bells, tray, bowl.

Moments of the Soul

Seeing the mystery close up
only deepens it. I wonder at
the peeling sheep, the Nikes,
the cracks and chips, the black
nails of the altar-boy mechanic's helper–and
the boys' rapt faces. For being late,
for being marginal, there are sometimes
compensations, maybe even gifts.

# Silence and Stillness

Terry Quill

# Musings

*Photography by Paula Basile*

The Leshan Giant Buddha is the largest carved
stone Buddha in the world, and at the time of its
construction (during the Tang Dynasty),
it was the tallest statue in the world.

# Coat Sleeve Pratapana

Carly Sachs

*for Devarshi*

Imagine a thousand snow globes of every place you've
ever been,
all that you've tasted, all that has moved you,
all that you have loved.

Good pilgrim, shake all that glitter inside you
re-awakening your own inner magic
a thousand worlds shining through you

and as you return to stillness
notice who you truly are in this moment.

*Winner, Third Place*
*Spirit First Poetry Contest 2010*

# What is the Question?

Cynthia Anderson

*The last of the human freedoms is to choose*
*one's attitude in any given set of circumstances...*
*~Viktor Frankl*

Strong winds blow in from the backcountry,
bearing ash from a wildfire long cold.
The fine gray haze obscures sky and sun,
proof that events we thought were over
follow us into the meditation loft
where we sit inviting our minds to be still.
Woodpeckers drill straight into the building,
backhoes beep from the service yard below,
loose metal flaps against the roof.
Vast questions like *Why are we here?*
shrink to *How can we stand it?*
Most eyes stay closed, willing to prove
that our minds can go blank for one second—
no matter how the world shocks us
or insists on uprooting our calm.

# Muktinath

Faith Van De Putte

The crows circle. They are bits of dust
pried from the hills, a teeming group
thrown by the wind, lifted
so their stark shapes
are script against the red monastery wall.

The wind comes up in the afternoon,
crawls out of the north and follows the river down.
The river is starved in this dry season, its banks hold
stones and thin water woven through.

Here the ridge drops to valley,
prayer flags catch wind in a tangle.
Some are bright new and others faded to an
unraveled and simple white.

How many months does it take
to release each prayer stored in those bits of cloth?
On windy days do the prayers fly down the valley,
catching on trees and thorny bushes? Do people find
them in drifts by the walls? Could you
catch one in your hands?
Would it chime in pure sound
or be only an unexpected thought?

And how long does it take for each prayer
stored in one's heart to let go and fly free of the self?

Moments of the Soul

Are we like those flags, slowly unraveling
dependent on the sun, the voracious wind to let our
goodness out?
Or are we the crows, intent in our own form,
asking the wind to help us home?

# For Ghosts Clinging to Trees and Grasses

Christopher Burawa


Thought is struggle. And what you call
life is thought. When thinking ends so
does the hum of needing to interpret
life, and so thinking is manifesting the hum
that interprets the place where you are.

Fear creates the hum when,
after a time, you forgot completely
the place you were last in and
remember that you were somewhere
else. And if this sounds like a dream, it's
because your mind is as if in a dream.

You struggle to get back but really
don't have to, because fear creates the
thought to go back and you do. Along
the way, it reassembles the past, interprets
how you last remember what happened

but is inexact. Then the cosmos breaks
open to let you through. Something is born.
Experience, sensation begins as if
reborn. You then remember the space
around you, and inhabit it.

# Being

Christian Williams

Being apart
is an illusion
we all share
together.

What is us?
What is we?
Is it the total?
And some of its parts?

My soul lives
In old
Hand-me-downs
From another wardrobe.

# En Route From Cozumel

Mary Harwell Sayler

The sea
        cruises
beneath us.

Ever the sun
makes blackness
        blue.

I cannot fathom
        the depths
to which Light goes
        to reach me.

# Consider Your Muse

Maria Wingfield Butler

Go with her, even in the dark,
to where she leads you.
If you've ever turned your back on her,
know that she takes
her subject by the hair
but only if you're considered worthy.

There'll be no light,
and the ground you walk
pocked with holes.
Stumble along and listen for the
distant singing that lifts the dawn.

When the first smear of light appears
space opens up.
You won't just see, you'll know.

The wind is sweet to taste,
the sea has silver on it,
babies, instead of wailing,
hum a special pleasure at
the mother's breast.

It won't be *all* sweet but sweeter than
you will ever know should you
divorce your servant and leave her
folded in the shadows of your heart.

# Take Heart

Jan Keough

Nothing is ever lost
or mislaid
even by you.

From alpha to omega,
the trail of you is etched
into each equation.

The cosmos cannot forsake
its essence.
It will not lose you.

Take heart.

Every beam of light
rejoices
with the prism's touch.

So we radiate
one to another
in a heart's glance.

Our innermost selves
echo like footprints
on unswept shores.

Beyond tomorrow

and past today
we share familiar orbits.

Yesterday watches
for our return -
sometime, anytime.

So that nothing is ever lost
or mislaid
even by you.

# Meditation #4

Caits Meissner

When you feel pulled in too many directions
and depleted, lay down with your legs spread wide apart.
You are birthing the world and it slips from you
easy as water.
Out pours a storm of taupe and turquoise and
magenta and lava, otherwise known as love, or creation.
These are things that cannot be explained in human
tongue. We have been seeking for centuries,
chasing the daunting mystery of the immortal spirit.
Do not be afraid, great one, for this is your power,
winking stars and swirling gas, smooth stones to grab
from thin air to rub between fingers, cool and soothing
to touch.
A ball of light that might be the moon
suspends over head like a halo. Feel your body hum.
Embrace each vibrating planet, including your skin, that
long organ protecting the raw bits.
You stealthy creator, you. Beckoning existence
from your most damp, wet place. Becoming God.

# Ahimsa

Carly Sachs

*for Brian*

Ahimsa sounds like wind, a soft sigh or breath,
the way wheat moves in a field

or the way sun warms the body,
how much it comes in waves, one and then

another and another, always another chance,
a time to ride, feel, and be alive;

in this way, it is always a continual practice,
much in the way blood is always being circulated in the
body.

Or, it can be like light, like the one in a dark café,
airplane or bus, the one that helps you find your page

or your place. Ahimsa is the word you write, or say when
you need to find meaning. Ahimsa is the breath

that whispers in your ear, that inner voice or teacher
who tells you, you are loved.

# How to Get There

Alexander Russo


Discard any drags.
Leave all arguments behind.
Don't pack worry or doubt.

Be prepared to discard voices
telling you it's a hopeless journey.
Give up all habits, even good ones
until you're hollow as a reed.

Streamline yourself to eliminate friction.
Try running with the wind, look back.
If you see a cloud of dust, run faster.

If you're successful
you'll be running faster than time
and will catch up with your former self.

Before it can trip you, nudge it aside.
Keep going until you enter
a place of brilliant blinding light —

a metaphor for another metaphor
no one can explain —
but you'll know you've arrived.

# Say Yes

Melinda Coppola


OK, listen up
I'm only going to say this once
An hour. Hourly I'll speak until the truth of it
So saturates your knowing
that it's all you know and all you'll ever
know for sure. For you are surely and certainly
everything you think you lack.
Be certain of this, in the soul of your soul,
that place where the still pond waits
like a lover, to come home to over and over and
to slip into like a deep silent dream, that quiet water
reflecting your grace.
You lack nothing. You are everything.
You are everyone you love, loved, are about to.
Love, that is.
Love that is a mirror in which
when you love,
your own perfection is held up to your smiling eyes
like an engagement gift from God.
Say yes. Say yes. Say yes.

# Hermits

Gabriel Griffin

Like slaters that poke their heads
in and out of caves, they burrow blind
into a vast theological darkness, losing
the dried crust of their thoughts, bumping
into gods.

When they emerge they are
shell-less, naked; no scales, no
defence of fur or hide; soft things, amorphous,
sticky still with dreams,
leaving shining trails.

# The End of Suffering

Stephen Cribari

*(After Catullus, Bro. Maurus, and Tensin Gyatso)*

The end of suffering is possible
The end of delusion is possible
Nothing is possible, in my mind

Hold me within your great compassion
For there will come a time when I must leave
Already my spirit quivers in my flesh like a bubble in
water
And death will be quick to strike. And yet

In the place behind my eyes I see sunlight shining on sea-
foam
Above my shoulders I feel the wind
My neck is warm with a vast stillness under an empty sky
And in the place opposite my heart I hear bells

Hold me within your great compassion
That I may quiet my wanderings
And unroll my life from my heart without fear

Hold me within your great compassion
For the end of suffering is possible
The end of delusion is possible
Nothing is possible, in my mind

And for the pilgrim, nothing succeeds like nothing

# If There's a Resurrection

Temple Cone


If there's a resurrection, it won't have music.
Music is the soul's longing for resurrection before it
comes.
If there's a resurrection, every creature shall grow wings,

And larks, partridges, and vireos shall become imams of
flight.
If there's a resurrection, the crows won't be invited,
But shall bear night on their backs, as they did from the
beginning.

If there's a resurrection, fields of clover shall invite us
To dance till our bodies shatter in an ecstasy of summer
rain,
Then raise our own white crowns to the chromatic
aurora.

If there's a resurrection, the names of things again shall
signify.
Barley shall be barley, feather feather, river river, and
bliss—ah!
Though if there's a resurrection, the light shall go on
speaking its name.

The priestly portions of the soul shall dwindle if there's a
resurrection,

Being metaphysical vestiges, our spiritual coccyx and
appendix.
But if there's a resurrection, the true priests won't lament
this change.

If there's a resurrection, God shall join us quietly by the
fireside.
From his hands tumble flowers of amen as intricate as
Persian epics.
From his lips pour waters of forgiveness, which he too
shall drink.

# When

Melinda Coppola

When all the talking is over
When sweet the silence is here
When all the reaching is finished
When clouds of illusion clear

When ranting becomes old-fashioned
When resistance drops away
When the body's urges quiet
And we let that quiet stay

When boundaries between, dissolve
When heart is one with mind
When past and future exit
And by clear light we find

That truth as we believed it
Was never true at all,
That Busy-Mind constrains us
Divides us, makes us small

When all the words are finished,
When all the knowing ends
There's only one real tenet
Upon which truth depends

That **anything** received with awe
In the moment's fleeting embrace

Moments of the Soul

Expands to guide and lead us-
We are eternal grace.

Moments of the Soul

# Gifts

Janet Rudolph

Isn't it enough to know:  The winds and the tides
Must we be reminded of our breath and our nourishment
as well?

My food, comfortably sating, is the dreamstuff of the sun
and the earth intertwined, the sun shooting out, the earth
accepting, creating sustenance and love.

And which in its power chooses to gift itself to me.

My water, flowing into and through my body, once flew
through the sky on wisps of clouds, floated to earth on a
glistening slide and journeyed
deep into the land.

And which in its beauty chooses to gift itself to me.

My air, quickening my blood, once swirled in the sky,
whirled in ocean currents and visited the very core of the
earth itself.

And which in its energy chooses to gift itself to me.

My vibrations, forming my essence and bringing me song,
once danced with the stars, hummed with the Milky Way
and chanted with the universe.

And which in its mystery chooses to gift itself to me.

And when I know, truly deeply know, I turn myself inside out to add my own essence.

And return the gifts.

Moments of the Soul

# Stuck in Traffic on the Henry Hudson Parkway at Sunset

Marie-Elizabeth Mali


Three Orthodox men are davening on the shoulder
next to their car. Like contemplative nuns

and sadhus in caves, the net of prayer
they weave—never for themselves—

could be what keeps this world limping along.
Maybe I'm not undone by the clouds

and sunset's flame because of their diligence.
Maybe they enable me to move through my day

barely noticing hundreds of sights
that would otherwise drop me to my knees.

# Visitation

Bo Niles


You knocked at the door
Entered the house
Removed your sandals
Washed our feet
Ate, drank, talked
With us so quietly
That when you left
Leaving crumbs
On the table
And a few drops of wine
In the cup
We didn't realize
That these
Were the silent signs
That would allow us
To go on
Without you

# Moment of Reflection

Carmen Mojica

I have come to conclude that my self is longing to
exclude all that does not matter in this matter of
being alive
That all the pleasures of the flesh are just distractions
from positive reactions to the events that occur to us
day by day
Some of us fail to exhale all the trivial and inhale the
greater scheme of things; that all this is just a
manifestation of a thought from a higher being; the
formation and creation of spirits that defy these petty
laws that obstruct and construct a diversion from the true
meaning of what it is to breathe

And some of us find it hard to conceive and believe that
all that functions and malfunctions before the devices we
call eyes is just not real; just because it has materialized
does not mean we shouldn't realize how this world is
simply another trial that our troubled souls are
experiencing;
For you see, we are all deities, musical notes that have
been composed and played in a bittersweet symphony by
the greatest composer of all time;

We are the most precious and golden intellections sprung
from a being so great that it is the perfection we strive
to achieve;
That we are just energies in a circle that truly never ends

Moments of the Soul

The secret to why our eyes cry and why we are alive, just barely, lies deep within the self that we often bury in layers of makeup just to collapse and rebuild and wake up to wander and squander our precious time, which in theory does not exist but rather serves to assist it who calls itself I am with the education of us
That we might be the wind in the door and understand that our mission is absolutely this and simply this: to learn what we forgot when we fell from grace and onto an unfamiliar face

That our ultimate goal should be to learn, educate and die; for it is in death that we are released into a peaceful eternity
So if anyone should speak to you of dying, know that dying is just the beginning of another lesson that is to ultimately just love unconditionally; just love because that's how simple yet complex it is
So if anyone should fear death, they are fearing a near-life experience

*Spoken Poem Winner*
*Spirit First Poetry Contest 2010*

# Meditation #7

Caits Meissner

the desert cactus grows against
the beating of sun & night's cruel chill

come morning, spread your limbs
beneath its thin shadow

break a stem and drink its water
your mouth, a sweet praise song

the distant air bends in heat
a single drop cries from left brow

you pour the cactus syrup into sand
and mix with finger mallets

it turns cool, compact and wet
perfect clay, you sculpt

the small pile of dirt insists on evolution
expanding upward, its nose to sky

come midday your palms run
against the long slope of a wall

by the hour when the sun's sunk its ship
it reaches tall as a house

the sun tips its hat and vanishes
you stand below a pyramid

dry and massive, a still elephant
crowned with a lonesome star

the opening you'd thought to carve
welcomes you in to rest your weary bones

a lantern shines inside, waiting for you
there is a woven mat to rest your knees against

and a book with your name on it, a pen
a bowl of ripe peaches to gift your teeth

a bucket for which to wash your face
you dip your aching finger in the warm pool

press your palms together
and pray

# Meditation
Wendy Winn

No real need for cathedrals
For ceremonies
For cloths, candles, wine or incense.
No real need for mosques
For rugs
For head coverings or prayers
No real need for temples
For sacred objects and icons.
You have all you need
Right inside of you.

Sit by the TV
Sit quietly in the car
Sit on a chair, on the floor, in a bath,
Sit alone, in a crowd, at the mall, in a stall,
Just sit,
Close your eyes and enter within.

Sit and with closed eyes, gaze at your third eye
feel the energy build there,
Feel your breath and let go.
Submit, submerge, give in and merge
Relax, let go, forget all you know
Be alone, be alone and slowly,
Become one
With all there is.

This is God, this is bliss, this is everything that is.
This is beyond what you have to understand or study,
You don't have to be saved or learned or chosen
Just go, be alone
And slowly become one
With all there is.
This is God, this is bliss, this is everything that is.
This is it, this is meditation.

# Let Your Yoga

Melinda Coppola

Let your Yoga
Walk with you in the hours
of your mundane days,
Remind you, Re-Mind you of
who and what you really are
Be your confidante
Hold you steady when the storms pummel your skin
Blanket you when the winter's chill would
crack your bones.

Let your Yoga
Cool the flames of your anger,
Keep your age a delight rather than a worry,
Love you when you can't love yourself
Take your hand and lead you along
when fear would have you freeze

Let your Yoga
Soften your hard edges,
Invite breath in when resistance would keep you back
Lengthen you when you can't reach the sun,
Strengthen you when you can't find your ground,
Coax your arms open wide enough,
Wide enough to embrace whatever the Universe wisely
sends
your way.

# Stepping Stones

Stephen Linsteadt

from the infinite intelligence
beyond comprehension
arises the script of desire
thought and deed
intertwining with our being
deceiving our believing
that we are the creators of our destiny

we remain unaware of the stepping stones of grace
orchestrating our life according to the cosmic plan
arising spontaneously
to meet our stepping feet

Moments of the Soul

# Meditations
# in the
# Natural World

*Photography by Wendy Winn*

# Stillness is like water
Judith Prest

Stillness is like water
moving deep inside the earth
seeping slowly between rocks
trickling down
in the dark
a tide moving inward

Stillness is the space
between breath
inside heartbeats
the silence of the gathering wave
that never breaks

Stillness blankets me
cushions me against my own
sharp edges
wraps me in her protective shawl
keeps my tender heart
from ripping
on the thorns
of the world

*Winner, Third Place*
*Spirit First Poetry Contest 2010*

# Recycling

Nancy Priff

Last winter's storm broke the old bones
of our oak hollowed by seasons passing.
Now in cleaning season, the hacking of an axe
fells in hours what nature took decades to raise.

Homeless wrens flutter, and a troupe of
acrobatic squirrels tumble to their next big top.
Without their living jungle gym, the children
turn to the cold metal bars of the schoolyard.

I am porous with grief, though I know nothing
is ever lost. When the wood is chopped and split,
I lay an armload in the grate. It leaps to blaze,
stretching its warm arms, exhaling its smoky breath.

Later, I scoop the ashes, sweep the bricks.
To the compost, I carry the leaden bucket of ash,
tipping to one side like a wind-whipped tree.

Where the old tree lived, two tiny heads press
green through the earth. Here, I spread the ashes,
recycling the old oak into the hope of new life.

# In the Church of the Cactus Forest

Rick Kempa

I too raise my hands above my head outspread
in the morning. Only I do not congregate,
vocalize a faith, resolve to carry the grim word
of salvation denied to the bleary-eyed.

Their sleep is beautiful. Arising at first light,
I tuck their blankets, touch their skin,
and go to the church of the cactus forest
for a communion best kept alone.

Maybe, later, I will relate something exotic:
how the boulders in a dark hollow
shifted at my approach, raised their snouts,
became the pungent *javelina,*

or how, when I entered an *arroyo*, the odors
of the dew-drenched desert conjured
that morning ten years ago of the great storm
and who I was that day.

But when the sun sheers the cloud bank
and bejewels each spindle, thorn, blade,
and the liturgy of the birds crescendos
and wings shimmer and the air thrills,

I stop, unlayer myself, take
the sacrament of the pen in hand, become

a vehicle, an organ of the near and far,
until I raise my arms and the pen falls...

Moments of the Soul

# Last Light

Drew Myron

*Cape Blanco, December 31, 4:53 p.m.*

*Located on the Oregon Coast, Cape Blanco is
the most western point of the contiguous U.S.*

We stand on the edge of earth
to study the horizon for last
light. This rolling western edge
swallows, surrounds.

On this last day, in pale
light we peel the skin
of a new start, vow
to say yes          quickly, kindly
talk less     listen more.

Wind presses memory,
cups an ear to the thin wall of hope,
answers every loud
cry, every sudden turn.
Calls *yes          maybe          wait.*

The sun sets, a faint
moon pulls. We dive
into all we know,
all we do not.

We spread our arms as the
smallest bird extends wings
and despite size
shoulders a trust that
hurts amassed will soften
with time, each day fuller than the last,
everything flies and forgives.

Moments of the Soul

# Between the Branches

Christian Williams


There is knowledge to be had
In this world.
Not like pouring liquid
In a bucket.
Not like collecting
Small round tokens.
Not like amassing anything.

Knowledge is admiring
Beautiful tiny veins
Of a small soft leaf.
It just left the tree
And now lives
Between these two fingers
Pinching it together.

Knowledge creates a smile
Aware that the leaf
Looks back.
We two have broken away.
We two are falling slowly and gracefully.
We two have touched
The earth.

The leaf turns over.
It shows its face
That sees through me,

The tree,
And the infinite blue
Lost
Between the branches.

Moments of the Soul

# Unseen, Unheard

Gail Denham

There's little we see – only the barest
outline, the briefest glimpse of something
so wonderful, so divine, we'd go blind
and likely expire if all were shown.

We hear a faint rustle of leaves, high
in the ancient elms. This time it's not squirrels
or nuthatches. A breeze touches your hand
as you reach for the rake.

Behind all this quiet beauty is such a swell,
such free joyous dance. Only the ripple
of a mole seeking a tulip bulb reminds
there's movement we can't know. Not yet.

# Pond in April

Ann McNeal

You crunched last-year's leaves
underfoot, down to the pond's edge,
sat in the clear spot at twilight
and the hush was a bowl
of soft light placed gently
over the water, bugs
skittering the surface, the gentle
high shish of the stream entering
and leaving by the beaver dam,
hemlocks bowing, and the high
dead snags holding up the sky,
one heron watching you with legs
astraddle. Slowly you painted
yourself into the picture, breath
dropping lower. There was
nothing more you desired,
nothing needed, nothing omitted
and not a thing happened
all that evening.

# where silence grows

Christina Beasley

i want to be still but not how
a dead thing is. not stale or pallid,
like worn paint. i want to know
the way that vibrancy can tiptoe
through the veins of my palms; serene
and cool, humming a song of smoke
and light.

there is a sweet rain that falls when
the cracked skull of streambeds murmurs
for touch. the meditation of something
opening, the reveal, will only reverberate
if an ear is pressed to the ground.

i swear, that night, i watched willows
eek from fissures. a vine throbbed out
of a crevice of soil and sweat. the dew
of wildflowers knocked on a ground
of glass; reticent. a marvel, and all
was silence but the strumming of their roots.

# A Respite in July

Roy A. Barnes

Standing, caught between
June's drought and August's swelter
-drenched by heavy rain

I meditate here-
My parched soul finds amnesty
from its dry season

Moments of the Soul

# Earthchild

Margaret Kirschner

I'm a child of the earth
daughter of a farmer
whose thick-muscled fingers
crumbled clumps of dirt
lifted them to his face
to inhale
to nourish his very being
as his husky voice whispered
"Now that's fine soil."

Now his body
lies deep underground
enriching the earth.
When I tend his grave
the dirt sifts through my fingers
I lift it to breathe in its smell
I whisper
"Now that's fine soil."

# AMness

Darrell Lindsey

I have found a fragrance
in meditation tonight,
every breath of mind
inhaling the beauty
of innumerable roses.
I slowly read the moonlight
in branches of tall pines,
let their poems enter
into the stillness
as I become nothing,
and yet part of everything.
Before journeying to mountains,
perhaps I should rest a while
beneath a willow
beside the old pond,
try to sing a Rumi poem
from the arc of memory,
wait for ripples
in hearts on myriad shores.

# At Ribbon Falls

Rick Kempa

Desert water
working a seam
in granite,

carving a niche,
widening it,
buffing the surface:

something not to be seen
in passing, something
deserving wonder.

I have a plan
and a time span.
Someone will be

expecting me.
But this place asserts
its own imperative:

To sit in full sun
beside a boulder
in a pocket of sand,

water tumbling from above,
doglegging around me,
diving down.

To take off my hat,
bare my scalp, forehead, nose,
take off my boots, my clothes,

so that the sun can touch
every part of me—
It will not hurt me.

To take off my glasses
so that the light
flashing on the water's back

refracts into my eyes as heat,
and I cannot see to write.
To savor an apple.

To close my eyes
and tilt my face
toward the sun

like the lizard
on this rock.
To be still.

# Reflections on a Campfire

J. J. McKenna

*Upper Cataract Lake, Eagles Nest Wilderness*

The early evening moon, fresh-faced
and just beginning to wane, must be weeping
for suddenly dew appears on everything,
and in the deepening night, the campfire
retreats until, almost without heat,
it exhales a final plume of smoke.

Life's like that: a brief encampment, a bivouac
against the night, and like the campfire,
at first it smokes a little, then gives off a goodly heat,
and then declines to cold, dark ash.
And all the while those sister spirits, Water and Air,
wear away the mountains, and ancient Night,
that grand dame, reclaims her sable estate.

# Spirit of the Wind

Marylee Byrnes

The wind has secrets to tell you
although it cannot spell or even
pronounce what it whispers…
it only wants to be heard like a sigh
that breathes life into your soul…
try not to define it…
but simply let it carry you
to the mystical moving force
you have always known –
yet still need to discover.

# Sometimes

Gail Denham

Sometimes a wind squeezes
through a window, and brushes
hair from my forehead. I welcome
its voice that whispers secrets of hikes
in the hills after church, our jackets
soon piled on Mom's arms, climbs
to peaks of rocks where we posed
for Daddy's slow camera, and watched
colors change on rocks
that we didn't love then.

# On a Path

James Eric Watkins


hovering within
a moment, I found
god today, on a path
in the forest, under
a lush green canopy of leaves

the light peeking
through the silence
and the sound of song birds . . . singing
beauty coming into focus
harmony into balance

it was there, next to a tree
draped in snake-like vines
wrapping around my mind
the smell of warm honeysuckles
thick in the air, it was there

standing still, that I found god.


*"I loafe and invite my soul."*
*~ Walt Whitman*

Moments of the Soul

# The Owl and the Meditator

Krista Kurth

In the midst of meditation,
Sinking into silence
Under the setting sun,
Comes the haunting hoot
Of an obscure owl
In the nearby autumn woods –
Whoo, whoo, whoo!
Echoing the quiet question
Resonating in the recesses
Of my primordial mind,
Who, Who, Who,
Am I?

As the sound subsides
The ripples of peace left
In my awareness answer
The timeless inner inquiry
In my wise woman's soul.

# Tree Dreams

Lisa Dordal

Nothing but green-leaved branches
of a full-frame tree –
coming, from every point, a fabulous light.
As if one small edge has been lifted slightly –
a tiny tip of hem gathered –
to show the numinous beneath: the holy
underpinnings of world. Too much,
my lids break in joyous start.

# Altars

Judith Prest


I am remembering altars everywhere
flat shale of a creek bed
spread out to receive falling water,
sun through purple glass
on my kitchen window sill

I remember moss patches
in the Delaware woods like miniature
pine forests under the oak
and the great steps of granite
supporting the railroad bridge
blocks of stone
still sunwarm
when I sat meditating
on summer evenings
before I knew what meditation was
before I could claim it as prayer

I am remembering prayer bundles
bright cloth tied in the spindly alder trees
at the foot of Devil's Tower
the labyrinth at Stillpoint
where prayer connects my feet
to the spiral path

Earth herself is my altar
where I can feel

God's pulse beating,
hear in my own heart
faint echoes of the divine

# Holding a stone to my ear and listening

E. Jade Lomax

Round, flat skipping stones I find
in the bottoms of whispering streams,
communing with minnows and fire-orange newts.
I can feel the ground underfoot,
the earth turning beneath me.

I tie my words to heavy rocks,
drop them into wells of memory and
listen for them to hit bottom.
I'll dig them up, later,
like sunken treasure,
when I need them to fight monochrome days
and nights when I can't keep the cold out of my bones.

Sometimes the sky above me is grey.
Sometimes I forget that grey is beautiful.

Get your hammer and chisel
and go up on the flat mountain top.
Carve out ten stone tablets
and name them all love.

Remember dry red leaves against a charcoal sky,
branches like reaching hands you want to hold.

Remember flowers growing out of moss growing out of
fallen trees.
Remember how kelp forests rise from a life-bedecked
ocean floor,
when you're breathless, forty feet under,
and how the sunlight filters down like a gift.

Remember that you can't ever count the stars.

Write it in stone.
Never forget.

# Sparrows

Deborah Straw

Sparrows are not a celebrity bird.
People think they're common, dull.
No flashy colors. No bright patches of crimson or gold.
They wouldn't win a beauty contest (neither would I).
But have you listened to a sparrow's song lately?
Have you studied the variety of their brown and white
striping, sizes, habitats in your Peterson's guide?

Mine lists sixty-two varieties
with names befitting royalty:
Pine-Woods, Dakota Song,
Golden-Crowned, Macgillivray's Seaside,
names that transport me to meadows,
thick woods, shorelines.

As I pass half a century,
I find the common, the humble, the unpretentious
comforting.
I am not attracted to bright colors, in-your-face people.
In a crowd, I'm drawn to the quiet ones,
ones with complex stories behind ordinary faces.
A few wrinkles and bulges increase their appeal.
I am not so impressed by great beauty.

In the bird world, if given the choice
of the brilliant blue of the jay,
the piercing red of the cardinal,

Moments of the Soul

the raucous blackness of the crow,
I'll take the friendly spirit,
the small song, the dependability
of the sparrow.

Moments of the Soul

# Into the Sun

Chris Helvey

Sunday morning,
sitting
in silence
on
stones
beyond ancient,
staring
at the mirrored
surface
of Slick Creek,
trying to decide,
when I hear
them coming,
honking
and flapping,
flying
low and hard,
like hell
itself
was
after them,
a V of
Canada Geese
swoop
down
until
they are almost

in the trees,
then whirl and
rise
and
fly
straight
into the sun.

I turn
and watch
until
the final
black wing
is absorbed
by the light.

Then
I push
off
the stones
and
follow.

# In This Air the Eye Travels

J. J. McKenna

*Eaglesmere Lake, Eagles Nest Wilderness*

In this air the eye travels naturally
toward the far shore of Eaglesmere lake
to see Eagles Nest peak stand in duplicate,
a jacket of snow thrown over its shoulders
and its flanks draped in the Alpine green
of late, late spring. In the pure lapis sky
a cumulous cloud foretells the coming monsoon.
A rising wind sighs through the lodgepole pine,
and nearer to the eye a wild rainbow
dimples the glass as it dines on caddis flies.

Eventually I retreat from the lake's shore
and find a seat on a granite slab warmed by the sun.
Almost unbelievably I have this scene
all to myself—no sound or sign of another traveler.
For a time, then, all this beauty, all this silence mine.
I recline on a great boulder bed and pull my cap
over my eyes and doze a little as the day declines.

Then, only half aware, I hear a distant rumble
and look to see a pair of jets inscribing contrails
into the sky—one hurrying east toward the dark of night,
one chasing west as if in frantic quest of the sun.
In the time required for me to ascend two thousand feet
along the trail, those passengers, strapped in their seats,

Moments of the Soul

will reach another time, another place, completely foreign.
So I'll stay here, in this air, where the rock
warms in the sun,
where each spring this ancient peak
gives birth to the stream,
where always this azure tarn
reflects the amaranthine sky.

Moments of the Soul

# About the Poets

**Liz Ahl** is the author of the poetry collections *Luck* (2010, Pecan Grove Press) and *A Thirst That's Partly Mine* (2008, Slapering Hol Press). She lives in New Hampshire where she is a professor of English at Plymouth State University.

**Cynthia Anderson** is a writer and editor living in Yucca Valley, California. Her poems have appeared in *The Sow's Ear, Café Solo, ArtLife, River Poets Journal, Stone's Throw, The Sun Runner Magazine,* and others. She has received poetry awards from the Santa Barbara Arts Council and the Santa Barbara Writers Conference. Her collaborations with photographer Bill Dahl are online at www.rainbear.com.

**Mary Elizabeth Anderson** is the author of *Seasons of Hope: A Poetic Guide to Healing and Renewal* (www.MaryElizabethAnderson.com).

**Roy A. Barnes** writes from southeastern Wyoming. His poetry has been featured at Skatefic.com and in *Poesia, Pond Ripples Magazine, Conceit Magazine, joyful!,* and other publications.

**Christina Beasley** is a creative writing and international affairs student at Sarah Lawrence College. She has done writing residencies at Atlantic Center for the Arts as well as Southern Illinois University, and she read in the Washington, D.C., Miller Cabin Poetry Series in July 2010. She finds beauty in all things, including in her Venus Fly Trap collection.

**Christopher Burawa** is a poet and translator. His book of poems, *The Small Mystery of Lapses*, was published by Cleveland State University Press in 2006. His translations of contemporary Icelandic poet Jóhann Hjálmarsson won the 2005 Toad Press International Chapbook Competition. He is the Director of the Center of Excellence for the Creative Arts at Austin Peay State University in Clarksville, Tennessee. Burawa has been a disciple of Kyozan Joshu Roshi since 1994, and he is an ordained monk.

**Maria Wingfield Butler** is the Central Region Vice President for The Poetry Society of Virginia. She has three times won prizes in the PSV's annual poetry competition. Her poems have introduced documentaries and have appeared in *The Clinch Mountain Review, Military Lifestyles, A Commonwealth of Poetry* and *Jungian Venture*. She has taught children almost everything with the use of poetry for over 20 years. In 1996 she founded the Richmond Waldorf School. Butler's grandmother recited poetry the way most people engage in conversation. Her husband of 40 years and her two children have taught her or caused her to learn about 90% of what she knows or claims to know.

**Marylee Byrnes** is a resident of San Francisco's East Bay and a member of the California Writers Club. She published light verse for many years and is now working on a chapbook. Marylee is retired from office work. Email: marylee123@att.net

**Temple Cone** is an associate professor of English at the U.S. Naval Academy. His first book of poems, *No Loneliness*, received the 2009 FutureCycle Poetry Book Award, and his second book, *The Broken Meadow*, is due out from Old Seventy Creek Press in 2010. He lives in Annapolis with his wife and daughter. Visit his website at www.templecone.com.

**Melinda Coppola** has been writing since the age of ten. Her work has been published in several books, magazines, and other periodicals including *Harpur Palate*, *Kaleidoscope*, *The Autism Perspective*, *Welcome Home*, and *Celebrations*. A Yoga teacher and Reiki Master, she enjoys infusing her work of heart with her voice as a poet. Melinda is owner and founder of Spectrum Yoga Studio in Norwood, Massachusetts. She has a special interest in bringing the gifts of Yoga and Reiki to individuals with developmental disabilities and to their families. Melinda lives happily with her husband Nick, her daughter Emily, and a couple of well-loved pets. poemsplease@aol.com.

**Stephen Cribari** teaches law at the University of Minnesota Law School. www.law.umn.edu/facultyprofiles/cribaris.html His recent poetry includes *Massage Therapy* (CHEST, 2010); *Running with the Herd* and *The Death of Hugh* (CENTUAR, 2009); *It Seems a Lifetime Away* (DAMAZINE, 2009); *You Should Have Seen It* (2006 TIGERTAIL and 2007 BEST OF TIGERTAIL). His verse play *Fingerprinting a Corpse* appears in THE PLAYWRIGHTS' CENTER MONOLOGUES FOR MEN, ed. Kristen Gandrow and Polly K. Carl (Heinemann, 2005) 0-325-00742-X.

**Lorri B. Danzig**, M.S., C.S.L., holds a masters in Jewish Studies with a focus on aging and has completed professional training in compassionate care of the dying. She currently teaches a trans-denominational program to Elders focusing on the spiritual tasks of life completion. When she isn't teaching, she is fully engaged in the writing of a memoir dealing with a recent year of recovery and growth.

**Michelle Demers** holds an M.F.A. in poetry from the Vermont College of Fine Arts and has been published in *The Café Review, River of Earth and Sky, The Auroran, The*

*Burlington Poetry Journal, Collecting Moon Coins II, Diner, The Dryland Fish, The Blue Fig Review* and other publications. Her chapbook *Epicenter* won the 2006 Blue Light Poetry Prize. She teaches poetry and writing at the Community College of Vermont and Vermont Technical College. Regionally she also leads her own workshops, First Thoughts Writing Workshops. She lives and writes in Williston, Vermont, with her brilliant husband and exceptional cat. She is inspired by Vermont's spectacular countryside as well as the deep spiritual questions of life.

**Gail Denham** has been published in a variety of national and international publications over the past 30 years. Although her focus is now (mostly) poetry, her work has been in the form of short fiction, essays, news articles, and poetry. Gail's photography has appeared on the covers of books and magazines as well as in magazines, newspapers, and calendars. She conducts writing workshops at Northwest conferences and is a member of several state poetry associations, winning some contests. Her third chapbook *DANCIN' THRU' PUDDLES* came out in 2010. Gail Denham and her husband have 4 sons and 14 grandchildren—the delights of their lives, and gist for her writing mill.

**Gill Dobson**, born in Zimbabwe, is now living and working in the KwaZulu Natal town of Pietermaritzburg in South Africa, where she is the communications director for African Enterprise, a Christian evangelistic organization. Gill has a passion for poetry, art, photography, the beauty of nature, and the warmth and endless variety of the people of this corner of the African continent. She can be contacted by email at gilldobz@gmail.com.

Moments of the Soul

**Lisa Dordal** received a Master of Divinity degree from Vanderbilt Divinity School in 2005 and is currently enrolled in Vanderbilt's Master of Fine Arts program for Creative Writing (in poetry). Her poetry has appeared in the *Journal of Feminist Studies in Religion, Bridges: A Jewish Feminist Journal, Poems & Plays, Georgetown Review* and the New World Library anthology *Dog Blessings: Poems, Prose, and Prayers Celebrating Our Relationship with Dogs*. Her poem "Commemoration" was awarded the 2009 Betty Gabehart prize at the Kentucky Women Writers Conference and her poem "A Dream for the Earth" was a co-winner of Vanderbilt University's 2010 Academy of American Poets Prize. She lives in Nashville with her partner Laurie and their three greyhounds.

**Bill Frayer** is a retired college professor who lives and writes in Chapala, Jalisco, Mexico. He has published two volumes of poetry since arriving in 2007. He finds it easier to live mindfully in Mexico, in a beautiful mountain climate among gentle and generous people. He produces a blog about his Mexican experiences: http://mainetomexico.blogspot.com.

**Caitlin Gildrien** lives, farms, and writes at the feet of the Green Mountains, where spring is the fiercer side of winter, and summer just time enough to catch your breath for fall.

**Mary Gilliland** lives in Ithaca, New York, where she serves on the board of Namgyal Monastery Institute of Buddhist Studies, the North American seat of His Holiness the Dalai Lama. Her poetry has appeared in *AGNI, Chautauqua, Hotel Amerika, Notre Dame Review, Passages North, Poetry, Stand, Tygerburning,* and *The & NOW Awards: The Best Innovative Writing*. She was a featured reader at the 5th International Al Jazeera Festival in Doha, Qatar.

**Gabriel Griffin** is the 2001 founder and organiser of the *Poetry on the Lake* competition, festival, and events on Lake Orta, Italy (www.poetryonthelake.org and www.isolasangiulio.it ). She is also the editor of annual anthologies and the *Poetry on the Lake Journal*. She has been prized and placed in many competitions and published in magazines and anthologies from 1996-2010 (*Scintilla, Peterloo, HQ, Poetry Life, Acorn, Still, White Adder, Leaf, Envoi* et al.) Her own collections: *Campango and the Mouthbrooders* and *Transumanza* (www.poetgabrielgriffin.com).

**A. Jarrell Hayes** is the author of several novels and collections of poetry, including the novel *The Laroarian Conflict* and the poetry collection *100 + 1 Haiku*. He invites you to visit his website at www.ajhayes.com.

**Chris Helvey** is a writer, editor, publisher, and teacher. He lives and writes in Frankfort, Kentucky, and can be contacted at adobechris@hotmail.com.

**Mary Dyer Hubbard** is a Licensed Professional Counselor with the Samaritan Counseling Center. Earlier in her life, she was a nun and taught in poverty areas in the United States. She also worked as a college campus minister and as a certified hospital chaplain. Today she and her husband Carl Hubbard live in Horsham, Pennsylfania, where they enjoy playing guitar together.

**Peter Huggins** teaches in the English Department at Auburn University. His books of poems are *Necessary Acts, Blue Angels,* and *Hard Facts*; two new books, *South* and *Apocalyptic Images,* are forthcoming. In addition, he is the author of a picture book, *Trosclair and the Alligator*, which has appeared on the PBS show "Between the Lions," and *In the Company of Owls*, a novel for younger readers. For more information check out his website at http://phuggins.com.

**Veronica Bowman** is a poet and writer who wishes to provide inspiring, positive, optimistic ideas for others to ponder.

**Rick Kempa** is a poet and essayist living in Rock Springs, Wyoming, where he teaches writing and philosophy at Western Wyoming College. A book of his poems, *Keeping the Quiet*, is available from Bellowing Ark Press.
http://wiki.wyomingauthors.org/Rick+Kempa

**Diane Kendig** had her latest chapbook released last year: *The Places We Find Ourselves* (Finishing Line Press). Her previous poetry chapbooks include *A Tunnel of Flute Song* and *Greatest Hits 1978-2000*. Recently her poems have appeared in anthologies by NYU, Mayapple, and Bottom Dog Presses. You can find out more about her work at dianekendig.com

**Jan Keough**, originally from Boston, now finds that she's been in northern Rhode Island for many years. She has been enjoying yoga meditation for more than 30 years. Her poems have appeared in print and online including in *The River Poets Journal, New Verse News, The Providence Journal, Awaken Consciousness,* and *Lunarosity*. Her essay "Experiments" was broadcast on WRNI's *This I Believe* segment. Once upon a time, the Bay Area Poets Coalition awarded her 1st Honorable Mention for her poem "Lemon Life," a bittersweet story of a man, his marriage, and lemonade. Jan is a co-founder the Origami Poems Project, which freely distributes one-page, origami-folded poetry books to readers. Check out www.origamipoems.com—Jan's first attempt at website work.

**Margaret Kirschner**, 85-year-old mother of seven plus foster children, grandmother of seven, great-grandmother of six, returned to school to obtain her bachelors and masters in counseling in her late forties and early fifties. Her work in a chronic pain center and hospice has spurred her to take her writing more seriously. Her Buddhist practice and her life experience have prompted its spiritual content. The writing of Mary Oliver, Stanley Kunitz, Pablo Neruda, Hafiz, Rilke, Rumi, William Stafford, and Thich Nhat Hanh and the support of a loving friend and mentor have inspired her to focus on poetic language. Contact: kirschie83@gmail.com.

**Krista Kurth**, Ph.D., a former organizational consultant and executive coach and author of *Running on Plenty at Work,* is an aspiring poet and amateur photographer. She is inspired in her writing by nature, 30 years of meditation practice, and family relationships. She lives with her husband in the woods near the Potomac River in Maryland and can be reached at kkurth@comcast.net.

**Norma Laughter** is a photographer, naturalist, and former teacher. She is intrigued by the creative process and the role meditation plays in enhancing one's openness to possibilities. Norma says she writes because "I am both at odds with words and addicted to the dance." Her poetry has been best described by a reviewer of her most recent collection, *Tickle Grass and Toadflax*: "No obtuse, encephalitic verse here! Having refused to drink the kool-aid of literary elitism, Ms. Laughter writes with refreshing clarity." In 2009 her poem "The Mill Street Gang" won a first prize in *The Writer's Digest* annual writing competition.

**Wayne Lee** lives in Santa Fe, New Mexico, where he teaches at the Institute of American Indian Arts and runs a tutoring company. His poems have appeared in *New Millennium, The Ledge, The California Quarterly, New Mexico Poetry Review, New England Anthology of Poets, The Floating Bridge Anthology,* and other journals and anthologies. His chapbooks *Doggerel & Caterwauls: Poems Inspired by Cats & Dogs* and *Twenty Poems from the Blue House* (co-authored with his wife Alice Morse Lee) were published by Whistle Lake Press.

**Darrell Lindsey's** haiku and tanka have won awards in the United States, Japan, Croatia, Bulgaria, and Canada. One of his poems published in 2006 was nominated for a Pushcart Prize.

**Stephen M. Linsteadt** is a painter, poet, writer, and scholar of cosmology and consciousness. He has studied Eastern philosophy for over 30 years and has traveled to India to learn and gain experience about the spiritual path. Stephen is the co-author of *The Heart of Health: the Principles of Physical Health and Vitality* (Truth Publishing Co.). He is a published poet and has published articles on health, consciousness, and emotional well-being in various magazines, and he is a contributing writer for an international spiritual magazine. He is the co-founder of Global Alchemy Forum (www.globalalchemyforum.com), a community of poets, writers, and artists promoting workshops, weekly poetry salons, public readings, and exhibitions. Stephen's artwork may be viewed online at www.stephenlinsteadt.com.

**E. Jade Lomax** is a mechanical engineering major at UC Santa Barbara who spends her days watching methane gas bloom into flowers of fire in her morning chemistry lecture; writing Matlab scripts to predict the results of a zombiepocalypse; calculating the relative velocities and accelerations of various cars, trains, and planes; and scribbling numbers, peering at computer screens, and tapping calculator keys. Between linear algebra and dynamics, Ms. Lomax writes novels, webcomic scripts and a cooking blog; reads voraciously; studies Japanese and Spanish; swims; and takes long thoughtful walks.

**Iain Macdonald**, born and raised in Glasgow, Scotland, has earned his bread and beer in a variety of ways, from factory hand to merchant marine officer. He currently lives in Arcata, California, where he works as a high school English teacher. His chapbook *Plotting the Course* is available from March Street Press. rubricman@hotmail.com

**Marie-Elizabeth Mali** is a co-curator for louderARTS: the Reading Series and the Page Meets Stage reading series, both in New York City. For more information, please visit www.memali.com.

**Janet McCann**, a 1989 NEA Creative Writing Fellowship winner, has taught at Texas A&M University since 1969. Journals publishing her poetry include *Kansas Quarterly, Parnassus, Nimrod, Sou'wester, New York Quarterly, Tendril, Poetry Australia*, and more. She co-edited anthologies with David Craig, *Odd Angles of Heaven* (1994) and *Place of Passage* (2000.) She has coauthored two textbooks and written a book on Wallace Stevens: *The Celestial Possible: Wallace Stevens Revisited* (1996). Most recent poetry collection is *Emily's Dress* (2004, Pecan Grove Press). E-mail: j-mccann1@tamu.edu.

**J. J. McKenna** and his wife Barbara live in Omaha, Nebraska. They share a love of the natural world, especially hiking in the Rocky Mountains in the Alpine zone above tree line where the sacred earnestness and beauty of life are manifest. The spiritual cartographies of Taoism and Zen permeate much of his poetry. He is the author of *Wind and Water* (2010). His poem, "At the Japanese Gardens," was nominated for the Pushcart Prize.

McKenna is an award-wining teacher at the University of Nebraska at Omaha.

**Ann McNeal** lives in Pelham, Massachusetts. After teaching physiology at Hampshire College for three decades, she retired to write, dance, and paint. She credits Amherst Writers and Artists workshops for jump-starting her poetry. Her poems appear in *Equinox, Peregrine, Paper Street,* and other periodicals, as well as several anthologies. She spends a lot of time in the woods.

**Stephen Mead** is an artist, writer, and maker of short collage-films living in New York. His latest Amazon release, *Our Book of Common Faith*, a poetry and art hybrid, is an exploration of world cultures and religions in hopes of finding what bonds humanity instead of divides.

**Caits Meissner** Multi-disciplinary storyteller Caits Meissner uses an exciting blend of poetry, singing, music, performance, and visual art to deliver poignant testaments to the complexities of the human spirit. Caits has moved many audiences—from those on street corners to those at Columbia University, those at The Nuyorican Poets Cafe to those at Rikers Island. Winner of the OneWorld Poetry Contest, Caits attended the 2008 inaugural Pan-African Literary Forum in Accra, Ghana, where she studied under Pulitzer Prize winner Yusef Komunyakaa and other luminaries from the literary African diaspora. Find out more: www.caitsmeissner.com.

**Carmen Mojica** is a 24-year-old poet, writer, workshop facilitator, and model who was born and raised in the Bronx. She is a graduate of the State University of New York at New Paltz with a bachelor's degree in Black Studies and Television/Radio Productions. In 2009 she published a poetry chapbook entitled *I Loved You Once* and later that year also published her latest work called *Hija De Mi Madre* (*My Mother's Daughter*), a combination of memoirs, poems, and research material that not only explains the effects of race on identity from an academic standpoint but also shares her life as a living example. Carmen facilitates a series of seven writing workshops called "From the Inside Out" that focuses on self-reflection and introspection. She covers topics such as personal power and will; the muse in our creative lives; ourselves and our relationships; and self-evaluation. Carmen is currently pursuing doula certification through a fellowship program with Hudson Perinatal Consortium.

**Drew Myron** is a former newspaper reporter and editor who has also covered arts, entertainment, and travel for America Online's *CityGuide, Northwest Best Places,* and other publications. For over 12 years she has headed DCM, a marketing communications company. When not writing, Drew still enjoys writing—poetry. She won first place in the Tallahassee Writers Association's 2009 Penumbra contest and is the first to be awarded TWA's *Carducci Prize for Poetry*. She earned second place in the 2008 Pacific Northwest Writers Association's poetry contest. Her poems appear in *Beyond Forgetting: Poetry and Prose about Alzheimer's Disease* and various print and online journals. As a poet, Drew frequently collaborates with artists to combine the written word with visual art. In 2008, she teamed with artist Tracy Weil to create *Forecast*, a traveling exhibition of 12 horoscope-inspired poems paired with interpretive paintings. In addition, she hosts *Off the Page* writing/reading events, offers lively writing camps and classes for youth, and volunteers weekly with the Young Writers Group, a program of Seashore Family Literacy. Drew lives on the central Oregon coast and can be reached at dcm@drewmyron.com

Moments of the Soul

**Allene Rasmussen Nichols** lives in Dallas, Texas. Her poems have been published in regional and international journals and in the anthology *Dance the Guns to Silence: 100 Poems for Ken Saro-Wiwa.*

**Bo Niles** is a former magazine editor and writer who specialized in design and the home. She has written a number of books on home and design and has also written *A Window on Provence: One Summer's Sojourn in the South of France.* In her retirement, she has been taking—and loving—poetry workshops in New York City where she and her husband live. Her poems have appeared in *Ekphrasis, Avocet, Mobius,* and the *Episcopal New Yorker*, among others.

**Carol F. Peck** taught at University of Maryland for more than 30 years and conducted Artists-in-Education poetry workshops in schools beginning in 1971. She was Writer/Composer-in-Residence at Sidwell Friends School for 13 years. She has worked with at-risk teens, hospice patients, and prison inmates. Her publications include *From Deep Within: Poetry Workshops in Nursing Homes, "I Ain't Gonna Write No Pome!"* and several articles and poems in *Christian Science Monitor, Michigan Quarterly Review, Virginia Quarterly Review, South Coast Journal, Without Halos, Teachers & Writers,* and other journals. Her awards include an Avery Hopwood Award in poetry from the University of Michigan, an Excellence in Educational Journalism Award from the Educational Press Association of America, and a Distinguished Teaching Award from University of Maryland University College.

**Judith Prest** is a poet, collage artist, and creativity coach. She holds a certificate in Expressive Art Therapy from New York Expressive Arts Studio in Albany, New York. She began writing again in 1997 after a 20-plus year detour through grad school, career, marriage, and parenthood. Since her retirement from school social work in June 2009, she has focused on her "real work"—writing poetry, making art, and facilitating creativity and healing work in prisons, community agencies, retreat centers, and other venues. Her collection of poetry and essays, *Sailing On Spirit Wind,* was published in 1998. Her poetry appears in three anthologies and in several literary journals. Judith is a member of the International Women's Writing Guild, Hudson Valley Writing Guild, and the International Expressive Art Therapy Association. She lives in rural upstate New York with her husband, her 20-year-old son, a very large cat (Elvis), and a very old Labrador (Orion). Contact Judith at JEPrest@aol.com.

**Nancy Priff** has received a Fellowship from the Pennsylvania Council on the Arts as well as awards for poetry and fiction from Montgomery County Community College, The College of New Jersey, the Philadelphia Writers' Conference, and other organizations. Her poems have appeared in *Kaleidowhirl, The Hiss Quarterly, Triplopia, JAW Magazine,* other journals, and several anthologies. She holds an M.F.A. in creative writing from Fairleigh Dickinson University, and she is a freelance medical writer (nancy.priff@verizon.net) and voice-over narrator (www.voices.com/people/NancyPriff).

**Terry Quill** is an attorney and toxicologist who lives in Silver Spring, Maryland, with his wife Joan, son Ian, and dog Rocky.

**Christine Riddle** is a retired nurse living in Amherst, Ohio, where she and her husband reared three sons and a daughter as well as numerous four-legged family members. She is a work in progress, striving to be present in the moment, to find spirit near at hand, to trust intuition, to respect the interconnectedness of life, and to learn something new each day. Like-minded individuals are invited to contact her at christineriddle234@gmail.com.

**Janet Rudolph** is shaman-born! Through the traumas and pains of walking this beautiful earth, she forgot. And now she writes so as to remember.

www.flowerheartproductions.com

**Alexander Russo** is Professor Emeritus at Hood College, Frederick, Maryland, and former Dean of The Corcoran School of Art, Washington, D.C. His awards in painting include two Guggenheim Fellowships, two Fulbright Fellowships, the first Breevort-Eickenmyer Fellowship given in art at Columbia University, an invitational Visitorship to India under the auspices of The U.S. Indo Sub-Commission of Education and Culture, and an Edward McDowell award. He is author of *Profiles of Women Artists* (University Publications of America, 1985); *The Challenge of Drawing* (Prentice-Hall, 1987); *Vignettes*, his first poetry book (Morris Publishing, 1996); and *Poems and Images*, his second poetry book (Xlibiris Publishing, 2008). He lives in the Village of East Hampton, N.Y. He may be reached at P.O. Box 1377, Wainscott, N.Y. 11975 tel. 631.324.4914 and e-mail: cmdrusso@hotmail.com

**Carly Sachs** is a writer, educator, and Kripalu-Certified yoga instructor who specializes in using the practice to help those who are dealing with trauma. Drawing on her Jewish roots, Carly strives to adhere to the principle of Tikkun Olam, Hebrew for "repairing the world." She is the author of *the steam sequence* (Washington Writers' Publishing House, 2006) and the editor of *the why and later* (Deep Cleveland Press, 2007). Carly can be found online at thewhyandlater.com.

**Mary Harwell Sayler** is a highly ecumenical Christian, a lifelong Bible student, and a poet whose career as a freelance writer has resulted in 25 books of fiction and nonfiction and over 1000 poems, articles, and children's stories. Since 1983 she's also helped other poets and writers, first through her poetry correspondence course and critiques, and then through her blogs and websites, www.PoetryOfCourse.com and www.ThePoetryEditor.com.

**Deborah Straw**, who lives and works in Vermont, is the author of two books, *Natural Wonders of the Florida Keys* and *The Healthy Pet Manual.* She has published poems in several journals and magazines, but this is her first poem to be published in a book. As she ages, birds (and friends) become increasingly important to her.

**Faith Van De Putte** lives in a straw bale house on Lopez Island in Washington State. She is a gardener, massage therapist, godmother, and community organizer. For her, writing is an act of perception. She has had pieces published in *SHARK REEF, Labyrinth, Raven Chronicles,* and *Cheshire Review.* She can be contacted at faithelene@yahoo.com.

**James Eric Watkins** writes from Northern Kentucky. He has work forthcoming in *The Main Street Rag* as well as other publications. James's creative work has appeared in *Pegasus, Flutter, Word Catalyst Magazine, The Shine Journal, Off the Lake,* and many others. James is the editor/publisher of *Flowers & Vortexes, Creative Magazine,* and Promise of Light: www.promiseoflight.com.

**Anne Whitehouse** is a poet, fiction writer, essayist, journalist, and critic. She is the author of the poetry collections *The Surveyor's Hand, Blessings and Curses,* and *Bear in Mind* and the novel *Fall Love*. Originally published in 2001, *Fall Love* is having a second life as an e-book, with over 15,000 downloads. Anne Whitehouse's second novel, *Rosalind's Ring*, set in her native Birmingham, Alabama, was a finalist in the Santa Fe Writers Project Literary Awards. Her book reviews have appeared in major newspapers throughout the country. She graduated from Harvard College and Columbia University. www.annewhitehouse.com

**Christian Williams** grew up in Montreal, Canada, and now lives at the foot of the Appalachians along the Vermont border. He is a loving husband and father of two children. He teaches Visual Art in a small college and has been actively writing for over 30 years. He has published work in various anthologies in Canada, and he also has exhibited his art. Christian regularly practices Tai Chi and enjoys excursions in the local wetlands. He can be read at www.cwilliamsart.com and reached at cwilliamsartist@hotmail.com.

**Wendy Winn** is a freelance writer, translator, and artist living in Luxembourg. She has three school-age children, six rabbits, a very old cat, a master's degree in English, and a bachelor's in metaphysics. Wendy began teaching meditation in 2010; she is a graduate of Steven Sadleir's Self Awareness Institute and of Dr. Leon Masters's University of Metaphysics. Wendy is a former newspaper editor and journalist who continues to contribute to newspapers and magazines. She has written plays that have been performed in Luxembourg and published short stories and poetry in literary journals and anthologies in both the United States and Luxembourg. Wendy co-hosts a weekly radio show (The Corner Café, on ARA Radio), is a Reiki Master and practitioner, enjoys selling her art work to help raise funds for charity as well as pay back her huge art supplies expenses, takes rope yoga and theatre classes, and is a raw foods enthusiast. Wendy practices what she preaches and finds time most every day to be still and go inward. One of her favorite sayings is that when you're too busy to meditate, that's when you really should be meditating.

Moments of the Soul

# Our Photographs

**Marc Goldring (Cover Photo)** is a fine art photographer and author of *Discovering the Familiar* (2008), a merging of profound images and reflective poetic prose that inspires mindfulness in the reader. His images are presented on his website at www.marcoclicks.com. Marc is a Fulbright award-winning craftsperson and has had sculptural craft work displayed in galleries and museums nationwide.

**Cindy Lee Jones** is a self-taught painter and photographer who grew up in the beautiful mountains of northeastern California. She was encouraged by the women in her life and inspired by the natural beauty that surrounded her. Today she lives in the Palm Springs area with her husband Greg, and they have a beautiful daughter, Brittany. See her work: www.cindyleejones.com.

**Ashley Litecky** is a registered yoga teacher and holds a master's degree in clinical herbal medicine. She is an instructor at Tai Sophia Institute, is an owner at Deep Green Wellness, and is a clinical herbalist and yoga instructor at Blue Heron Wellness in the Maryland and Washington, D.C., area. www.deepgreenwellness.com

**Paula Basile** has a master's in human resources. She shares her Buddha photo with us from her world travels.

**Wendy Winn**—read more about her in our poet bios.

# Author Index

Moments of the Soul

Spirit First
P.O. Box 8076
Langley Park, Maryland 20787

www.SpiritFirst.org

meditate@spiritfirst.org

We'd love to hear from you about the poems in this book, about what moves you or inspires you. Contact us at meditate@spiritfirst.org. For information about our current poetry contest and next year's poetry book, check out our website at www.spiritfirst.org.

*Spirit First promotes the practice of meditation and the development of spiritual awareness and mindfulness, inclusive of all disciplines and faiths. We seek to serve by providing education, tools, and networking that support those on a spiritual path. Spirit First encourages holistic attitudes, healthful living, gentleness with the earth, and compassion with the world.*

Bodhisattva

Made in the USA
Lexington, KY
07 January 2011